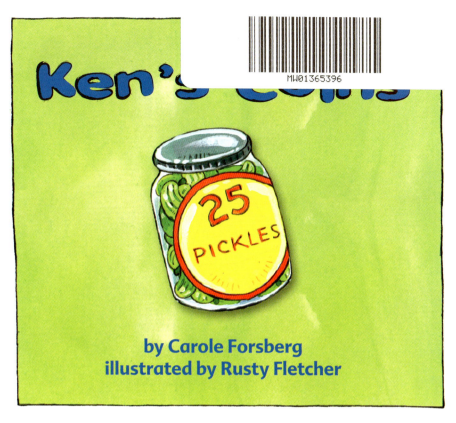

by Carole Forsberg
illustrated by Rusty Fletcher

HOUGHTON MIFFLIN   BOSTON

Copyright © by Houghton Mifflin Company. All rights reserved.

No part of this work may be reproduced or transmitted in any form or by any means, electronic or mechanical, including photocopying or recording, or by any information storage or retrieval system without the prior written permission of Houghton Mifflin Company unless such copying is expressly permitted by federal copyright law. Address inquiries to School Permissions, Houghton Mifflin Company, 222 Berkeley Street, Boston, MA 02116.

Printed in China

ISBN 10: 0-618-88668-0
ISBN 13: 978-0-618-88668-5

456789 0940 16 15 14 13
4500404709

This is Ken's favorite game.
Dad hides four coins. Each coin is under a clue.
Ken must find each coin by finding its clue.

Ken saw 5 apples in a bowl.
He said, "A nickel is here."
Ken was right.

What clue did Ken have?

"This is fun! I see another clue," said Ken.

"I know where the penny is."

4   Where will he find the penny?

"Where could the dime be?"
said Ken. "I see the clue!"

What clue does Ken see?

"Ha! I know what I will find under this!" said Ken.

6   What coin will Ken find under the pickles?

"What will you do with all your coins?" asked Dad. Ken smiled. "I'm going to hide them! I'll give you four clues," he said.

Responding

Math Concepts

Hiding Coins

Draw

Look at page 5. Draw the cans of soup you see.

Tell About

Predict/Infer Look at page 5. Tell how many cans there are. Tell what coin Ken will find under the cans.

Write

Look at page 5. Write the coin Ken will find under the cans.